Sonnets of Love and Silent Sorrows

A collection of Love and heart break
poems

Sohan Balaji SG

BookLeaf
Publishing

India | USA | UK

Dedication

To all the people who have enriched my life, imparted invaluable lessons, and guided me in discovering myself on this peregrination through my feelings and emotions.

Acknowledgement

The person who brought on the commencement of this book with a smile, my dear little sister, my little brother, and all the people who walked beside me on this journey through it all.

Preface

Love and heartbreak are profound emotions that leave lasting imprints on our lives. This collection of poems seeks to embrace both the euphoria of love and the ache of its absence, offering a reflection of moments we've all known.

Through these verses, I hope to stir feelings, awaken memories, and perhaps offer a sense of healing. Thank you for allowing my words to accompany you on your journey.

Falling out of love

She calls him and tells him,
"I love you, but I don't feel it anymore."
A thunderbolt splits his world apart.
He is perplexed.
He is puzzled.
He is trying to understand.
What it means.
"It's not you, it's me,"
She utters, "I love you, yet I don't feel
anything."
His world trembles, and he begs for her to
stay.
Who will tell that aching soul the ship has
long since sunk?
He fights to stay afloat on the last piece of log
left in the ocean.
As the waves of sorrow and despair drown
him in.

The Chase

The woman of my dreams
Loves the man of her dreams.
A love triangle, entwined,
Three souls bound by quiet suffering.
All three, tormented,
Finding solace in misery.
Knowing that the one they long for
Will never truly be theirs.
Yet they fight with swords of hope,
Battling destiny to change their fate.
While fate laughs in a corner at human grief.

Blind Man

I was lost within a dream.
There was this woman, as radiant as a
sunflower.
A woman I couldn't see, even though she was
right in front of me.
I wonder why?
Perhaps the endless search for something
greater blinds us to the beauty present right
in front of us.

A truly blind man is not the one who lacks
sight,
But the one who fails to recognize love.
A man who can't reciprocate and appreciate
the affection so freely given to him.
What does a man like that seek?
Is it sex? Is it companionship? Is it belonging?
Is it true love?
What renders him blind to the warmth of the
sun he feels upon his skin?
Maybe, this blind man is afraid of his skin
getting burnt due to the warmth he receives.

Not being able to digest the truth—that he
always deserved this.
Now he doubts if getting closer to this fire
will burn him to ashes or if it will keep him
warm enough to survive the winter he lives in.
Day in and day out.
The blind man pretending to be blind did not
want to see the beautiful world around him,
Because all he did was run away from the
aesthetics,
While always doubting and second-guessing
himself.
Wake up from this dream!
The world has seen enough blind men already.

I was always late

I was always late.
Late in confessing my feelings,
Late in telling them I wanted them.
Late in asking them to stay.
Trying to fight for my love,
Trying not to give up on my favorite human.
I was always late.
Late in stopping the search for something
better,
Instead of grabbing and never letting go of
what's in front of me.
Late in staying a little longer in a
relationship,
Late in finding time to make them feel
special.
I was always late.
For not fighting for what I always desired.
I was always late in trying to convince people
to stay.
Late in loving someone,
Late in breathing for someone,
In living for someone,

In dying for someone.

I was always late.

The Girl I Don't Deserve

How do I put this feeling into words?
There is a girl I love.
There is a girl I don't deserve.
Somebody as pure as morning light—
Naive, funny, fearless and complete.
I wonder what I did in my past life
To deserve someone like her,
To have someone like her by my side.
I wonder how will I live with myself when the
day comes,
Where I have lost her to the weight of my
own desires.
I will wake up as hollow as a tree that is
cleared for deforestation.
Yet I will live, Yet I will breathe.
Empty like a bag of flesh.
Long dead inside.
Maybe finding a reason to stay alive.
When my reason to stay alive is already long
gone.
Just like my breath will one day.

Butterflies

The butterflies had died.
He sat on his bed, motionless.
This feeling of absolute solace left him numb.
He knew not what happiness meant.
He knew not what agony meant.
All he understood was this unfamiliar
emptiness.
He sat there, wondering—what had become
of him?
Why doesn't he jump over the little joys of
life?
Why doesn't he cry anymore over the pain he
couldn't bear?
He had reached a state that others aspired to
be.
A state people called strength.
He wondered if having feelings for anything
in this world was a curse or a boon.
Is the ability to not feel anything a blessing?
Why do we run from what makes us human?
He laid there on his bed, looking at the
ceiling.
"Humans are strange," he thought,

As the rays of the sun entered his room.
This feeling of emptiness completely engulfed him.
There! Right there! Sat a sack of bones of flesh stitched together.

Turmoil

It was just for a fleeting day,
I was hers.
After all that turmoil we endured,
It happened, even though it barely lasted.
The idea of being hers was ignited.
Were we meant to be?
In search of love in the forest of beasts,
Waiting to pounce and eat each other out.
A sense of yearning lingered in the air.
Unexplored ground grew strangely familiar.
That feeling engraved.
That moment engraved.
That day engraved.
That thought engraved.
That love engraved.
Then came the barbarians,
Plundering, looting, ravaging to their heart's
content.
The once-flourishing forest was reduced to
ash.
Left barren, with no one to claim it

A devil incarnate

I met her again. She was radiant,
Happy, and loud.
She held my hand as we walked,
Her gaze locked with mine as we spoke,
She laughed with glee.
She let me know how much she missed me!
Forged lies with empty words, she spoke
about her options present out there.
In the constant pursuit of charming them, to
break their hearts just because her heart was
broken.
What are you?
A devil incarnate?
Are men merely play dolls to you?
She sips her coffee and smiles carefree,
Without knowing what she inflicted on her
victims.
I sat there looking straight into her eyes, A
chilling sensation creeping up my spine.
There she was—a master manipulator toying
with her puppets,
Moving her fingers of her own accord.

Letting me know about her jovial playtime
with her ragdolls.
There I sat, lost in front of this deceiver
Dumbstruck, smiling, too petrified to utter a
word.

Mirage

My voice cracked after the kiss,
I was left spellbound as I turned away.
I didn't know what to say, I didn't know how
to feel.
There she lay— a mysterious woman, forever
masked.
Who are you? What are you? What do you
want?
An array of thoughts swirled at the back of
my mind.
Why do you hide when you speak?
Why do you run from yourself when you
talk?
Why do you tell the truth, yet so casually
claim you're joking?
Why are you so impenetrable?
She sheepishly looks at me, nudging my arm,
Then takes a tissue and smudges the red
lipstick off my face.
Am I just another play doll to you? I wonder,
As I lay motionless, letting her wipe it off my
face.

The twisted tales of her past flicker before my
eyes.
As we got up and started to walk, I was lost.
Until she takes my hand as we walked from
the park.
Are these just empty words and hollow
gestures?
Crafted by a masterful manipulator?
And thus began our game of hide and seek,
From ourselves, from each other, and from
the world.
As we walked into the sunset,
I firmly held her upper arm knowing—
This was all just a mirage.

Twisted Love

Love?
Why is falling in love so terrifying?
Clinging to a fragile thread, desperately
backpedaling.
Trying to stay afloat, trying to retain what
you believe is forever.
Why is love so delusional?
A mirage that exists once you set your eyes on
the prize,
Only to wither away unnoticed, the glimmer
of hope that did exist feels empty.
Why is trusting someone so frightening?
Like the splinter of glass once broken in the
sandy beach, just lost.
Buried under the sand, hard to find.
Is it a curse? Is it a boon?
Will I ever know?
Until love ever exists beyond fleeting
moments,
I will cease trying to understand what love
truly is,
and perhaps, nobody ever will.

Sunshine

Sunshine? What does this word remind you of?

People? Place? Things?

Today, for me, sunshine reminded me of a woman.

An absolute chatterbox, with a large appetite for words, thoughts and feelings to be shared.

I used to think that I was the real sunshine on this planet.

Until I met her.

I don't remember the details of her tales distinctly,

All I remember is her talking non-stop without a pause to even catch her breath.

Take a breather, woman!

I'm not going anywhere.

She reminds me of my younger self back in high school where all he did was run his mouth like an enthu-cutlet.

Sunshine? Today, I felt you.

Your rays did reach me.

I think I finally understand what sunshine truly means.

I wanna feel it again.
Hopefully i get to feel it again.
That same feeling, that same warmth, that
same everything.

Love is a hoax.

Love is a hoax. *Bing, Bing*
It clouds your judgment.
Sting, Sting

Dazzles your mind. *Bling, Bling*
Chains your heart.
Cling,Cling

Breaks you like Kabir Singh.
Makes you flee like Milkha Singh.

Pulls at your hamstring,
And making you rest like a king.

A Tale of Fading Bonds

A tale of two strangers— bitter, sweet.
Are they even friends?
A soul in solitude, lost in a text.
Pestered by a wacko who longs for friendship.
They talk, they laugh, they eat, they play, and
they make merry.
Sadly did he know what destiny had in store
for him .
As All he longed for was a friend to confide,
tell a tale and jump with glee.
Days passed, things remained constant and
nothing changed.
Until one fine day, the thunder struck,
A thin crack surfaced between them ,
It spread its webs all over them, knowing not
the origin, The source nor the genesis.
The bond between the two souls withered
away like the seed heads on the white
dandelion.
The seed heads blown by a gust of wind, a
gust of breath, which they won't know.
A tall, invisible wall loomed over him,
Unscalable, unbreakable, unforgiving

A tale of two strangers bitter, sweet.
Were they ever friends?

The Pursuit of Love and Scars

Love? Affection? Care?
We humans crave these.
A pursuit to experience, attain and clasp it.
We embark on, why? Simply, just why?
Why can't we be content with ourselves?
Why can't we be at peace with ourselves?
Why do you need somebody else to give our
lives a sense of validation and happiness?
Humans are fascinating.
We seek the things we don't possess in others.
Thinking that the band aid will heal our
wounds.
Some self inflicted, some cross inflicted.
One day when the band aid is ripped off.
It hurts, it hurts far more than expected.
The temporary solution to the wounds we
give heals a little over time.
Yet the pain, the pain is still there.
It gives us sleepless nights.
We get used to it day in and day out,
with scars

To remind us of the conflicts we had.
These stay sometimes, forever.
As we engage in our pursuit of love and
happiness in others.
We hold on this fine thread to stay afloat to
escape from our past.

Flapping Broken Wings

I sat there on the sofa,
As she said she wanted nothing more from
me.
I was just an impulsive decision for her.
My heart sank, so all those conversations, all
those promises were just empty words?
Why is it so easy to discard humans so easily?
I lay on the sofa, my eyes closed, as tears
rolled down my eyes.
Sustenance is such a funny thing.
Even the right amount of love watered to the
plant to grow.
At the end of the day, it is absorbed by the
plant.
Until one fine day, it just wants to stop
growing.
You can't do anything, you're helpless, you feel
stuck, you feel dejected.
You ask yourself—
What does it really take ?
To make something last? Even when you are
perfect.

The world does not care, it's twisted.
Filled with complex human beings, Who cut
the strings when they no longer wish for the
bird to fly.
Not because they wanted to see it caged but
because they are simply tired of flapping their
wings with you.
Humans, love, decisions, can never be
understood.
Because all of them keep changing, they are
always dynamic.
Does forever even exist with someone?
I wanna experience it. I want to live it. I want
to breathe it.
I wanna die a thousand times within its
embrace.
I want it to burn me, consume me, and
destroy me.
But what a pity, as there is nothing as such,
That exists perhaps in this world?
But I don't wanna lose hope, I don't want to
sink.
I want to flap my broken wings to walk, even
If I can't fly like before.
In the end all you have is yourself.

The Gaze That Lingers

You see it. It sees you.
You don't break your gaze, nor does it.
Of all the mysteries in the world,
The gaze is the greatest mystery of all.
These eyes reveal stories unseen, unheard,
unrequited.
Our gazes interlocked, I see the emptiness in
your eyes.
Pitch black, yet you want to fight, yet you
want to be.
Searching for the small flame to light that fire
in you.
Yearning to be consumed by its flames.
That gaze tells a story of wanting, of being, of
knowing.
Yet we walk away knowing that's a far fantasy.
Those gazes still remember.
They return over and over.,
You lie there with no answers.
You don't want to know, you just want it to
be.
This endless game of hide and seek, this state

of chaos which only you two can understand,
but don't act on.
This suspense keeps me tethered, longing to
see you again,
hoping to experience this feeling again.
That one pair of widows you possess,
Through which I enter over and over,
Can I have them forever?

A Mortal's Muse

I sat beside her, my head resting on her
shoulder.
There lies this woman who is stupid.
Blind to sorrows of life.
Always living, laughing and breathing.
The curses of this world hold no power over
her.
She sings, she dances, and jumps with glee.
Why? What makes you celebrate life every
single day?
I wonder—what inflicts pain?
Maybe you feel it. That's why you appreciate
life for the way it is.
A brave soul walking on broken pieces of
glass.
Reminding me to live life to my fullest, cause
time peels us away closer to death.
We live as if immortal, we behave like it, we
eat like it, we pretend to act like it.
Until death strikes on our doors and we are
reminded that we were simply mere mortals.
Who will rot and die one fine day.

The Toy on Your Shelf

This urge to not text you back,
When every fiber of me longs to—,
This feeling is unbearable.
I guess, I have found comfort in this suffering.
I don't want to bask in it, even if it consumes
me whole.
And yet, I crave to relive it, day in and day
out.
I guess this is what it means to find comfort
in pain.
Once it becomes a habit you live and breathe
through it,
To a point where you become pain itself.
I don't want to text you back, because you are
simply used to toying with me with,
A set of toys you have present in your
cupboard.
I get to come out of the cupboard when all
your other toys are broken or not
functioning.
How can I describe this feeling to you?
I want to be played by you even if I am an

option.
In the end I will always remain your play doll,
Which you love toying around according to
your mood and requirements.

Pagal Aurat

What are you?
A pagal aurat, maybe?
To just conjure in front of my eyes to meet
me without any prior notice.
The women in my past never went to such
lengths to see me.Where I tend to ask
questions if you're crazy?
Why would you go so far for a person?
I despise traveling, it sucks the life force out
of me.
I don't know how you do it? Why you do it?
It just makes me feel special, I don't care! how
long this will last.
All I care about is just living in the moment
and breathing it beside you for the time
being.
Time does stop I guess when you indulge with
a rare bunch of people.
A woman full of surprises? How much more
can you surprise me?

The Coward's Awakening

What is this strange feeling? He felt it after ages.

A coward, who ran away from relationships of any kind, now clings on to one with a very naive woman.

I wonder! What does he see?

I wonder! What does he feel?

I wonder! How does he sleep?

Not letting her know the stories which his heart narrated.

He lived.

He lived every moment with her thinking this dream would end one fine day.

It didn't though, the lady had the greatest gift present in her, the power of having no ego.

This power was so powerful that the lady didn't realise that it won the coward over.

She never lost sight of him as he wasn't another human to her.

One fine day the coward wakes up from his deep slumber.

He was a coward no more.
He had grown into a man who wanted to love.
A man who wanted to feel.
A man who wanted to sleep drowned in her dreams.
A man who confessed.
Was it love? That turned the coward into something else? Who knows?